Execution Without The Drama
Copyright 2006   by Patrick Thean

Second Edition
ISBN 978-1-4116-8600-7

Gazelles Publishing.

Forward

Patrick Thean, a successful serial entrepreneur, is an expert at helping companies use dashboards to get your team aligned behind common goals, with a common tool, using a common language. The simplicity of his book makes it extremely powerful. Through his own story, he outlines the 9 Simple Rules for Dashboarding to help your company gain control and execute at peak performance.

The fundamental role of a leader is prediction -"whoever predicts better wins!" And a leader doesn't have to be years ahead, just days or weeks ahead of their market, competition, and team.

This ability to predict requires "headlights" that shine out further than the speed with which the organization is growing. Illuminating these headlights is data that provides a leader with insights sufficient to take advantage of opportunities and to avoid obstacles that can enhance or derail powerful visions.

The most successful growth companies are able to measure the right things to help them provide insight into the future of their business. How do they do this? They are committed to using dashboards to help them measure the right things, align all team members to a common goal and identify exactly what each team member needs to do to help achieve those goals. The visual and graphic nature of dashboards can be used as a communication tool to rally your team around critical objectives.

Head down the road of opportunity knowing that you and your team have the critical information necessary to navigate the turbulent challenges of growing a company.

Verne Harnish "Growth Guy"
CEO, Gazelles Inc and
Founder, Entrepreneurs' Organization (EO)

Contents

Introduction

The power of metrics is astounding! Actually, it's the RIGHT metrics that carry all the power. What can you measure NOW that will give you insight into the FUTURE of your business? I call this FUTURE VISION. Measuring the right things right now can help you predict outcomes. Predicting outcomes allows you to solve problems today instead of being blindsided by them tomorrow.

In the 1990's, I was running an Inc 500 company providing Fortune 500 firms with supply chain software solutions that reduced their massive freight budgets by millions. Growing in excess of 100% a year, with my "hair on fire", we measured various metrics including the usual suspects (such as revenues per head; revenues per customer; cost per employee) when it came to financial Key Performance Indicators (KPIs). But wait! These KPIs are about past and current performance. They allow you to celebrate with ice cream parties, but do not provide insight regarding future problems and outcomes.

It wasn't until I discovered the RIGHT things to measure that we began sharing bonuses as well as ice cream. This is my story, my journey of discovering the right things to measure and the dashboards that changed my future. Thank you for allowing me to share it with you.

Metasys, Inc.													3/11/2006		
Dashboard Report: Consulting													Quarter = Q4		
Goal/KPI	Owner	Unit	10/2	10/9	10/16	10/23	10/30	11/6	11/13	11/20	11/27	12/4	12/11	12/18	12/25
Client															
Referenceable	John	%	■	■	■	■	□	□	□	□	□	□	□	□	□
A/R Current	John	DSO	■	■	■	■	■	■	□	□	□	□	□	□	□
On-time, on-budget	John	%	□	■	■	□	■	■	■	□	□	□	□	□	□
Company															
Revenues/Head	John	$	■	■	■	■	□	□	□	□	□	□	□	□	□
Quality (Bug rate)	John	No.	■	■	■	■	□	■	■	□	□	□	□	□	□
Contractor cost	John	$	■	■	■	■	□	■	□	■	□	□	□	□	□
Employee															
Learning (Hrs/month)	John	Hr	■	■	■	■	■	■	□	□	□	□	□	□	□
Balance	John	Hr	■	■	□	□	□	■	■	■	□	□	□	□	□
Professional Growth Plan	John	%	■	■	□	□	■	■	■	□	□	□	□	□	□

Page 1

Execution Without The Drama™

My Jerry Maguire Moment

"It isn't that they can't see the solution.
It is that they can't see the problem."
~G.K. Chesterton

In the mid 1990's, I was running Metasys, a transportation logistics software company that I had founded in 1991. Metasys transformed the way a large company shipped their products to customers and in the process typically saved between 5% and 15% of their overall transportation budget.

Metasys was a rocket ship! We were growing at 100% each year and were ranked 151 on the Inc. 500 in 1996. We were working hard, playing hard, sleeping late and loving it. Our hair was on fire. These were both very exhilarating and stressful times.

Fortune 500 clients, the kind you really cannot afford to fail with - FedEx, Rubbermaid, Cisco Systems, and Levi Strauss and Company - these were some of the clients that we were blessed with. We had the typical weekly project status meetings that went over large project plans, deliverables, deadlines and issues. These meetings were laborious. The information was complex. When complex meets laborious, believe me, you don't get great outcomes. Yet, we had spared no expense in hiring top project management talent from the best consulting firms.

The Moment

It occurred the night I woke up at 2am in a cold sweat. I refer to this fondly as my Jerry McGuire moment. My gut told me that we were headed for a train wreck. But how could that be? I had recruited great talent and we were all dedicated to achieving the Metasys dream. We measured a number of financial KPIs regularly. In addition, I spent tons of time with our VP of Consulting on a weekly basis to review and assist on project plans and project issues. So how could we be headed for a train wreck? Should I dismiss this moment, write it off to stress, and go back to sleep? Going back to sleep was not an option. I was wide awake and my heart was pounding. I had to either validate my instinct and take evasive action, or prove to myself that I had nothing to worry about. What could I measure that would allow me to peer just a little into the future in order to avoid being blindsided?

My instincts told me that I already knew the answers. The only way to validate these answers was to first discover the right questions. But what were the right questions? The current questions we were asking gave us KPIs that helped us to understand how the business had performed. For that purpose, KPIs such as revenues per employee, revenues or profit per customer, provided an excellent history of past performance. Warnings of possible train wrecks down the line were a different story. For my purpose on this night, these were not the right questions.

Tip:
The only way to recognize a train wreck before it happens is to figure out what one looks like ahead of time.

The right questions would lead us to the *right things to measure at the right time.* If we had that data, we could then provide a system of communication and direction for the team.

RULE # 1

Start with the RIGHT questions

Our First Dashboard

I spent that night coming up with the right questions. These questions were translated into KPIs that provided us with our first forward looking dashboard, much like how headlights illuminate the road ahead for the driver of a car. Between the hours of 2am and 8am, I designed a dashboard with 3 categories containing a total of 9 indices. I used the word "indices" because I was not sophisticated enough at the time to refer to them as metrics or KPIs. **I called this a dashboard because I wanted to run my company by instruments, much like those a pilot uses to fly a plane.**

The three categories were Company, Employees and Customers. Each category had three indices. This dashboard was a spreadsheet with weeks across the top so that I could track new data each week and make decisions based on forward-looking trends.

Each index had 3 specific bands of performance color coded to Red, Yellow or Green.

Green meant that things were good.

Yellow indicated that we had encountered difficulty, and the difficulty could be resolved with some advice and help from management.

Red meant that we were headed towards a train wreck regarding the item that the particular index was measuring.

> **Tip:**
> Putting scores on subjective areas will make them more objective, resulting in less drama.

How an index was coded to red, yellow or green was quite specific. For example, take the number of hours that an employee was working on a project. If the team was working an average of 50 hours or less, that was green; 51 to 70 hours was coded yellow; and above 70 hours was coded red. What I did not realize back then was that I had just put an objective score on something that was very subjective.

The next morning I met with my head of consulting. To protect the identities of the innocent, we shall refer to him as Jack. I asked Jack to inspect all our projects according to these indices and deliver the results to me by the next morning. Jack was shocked by this new non-billable assignment, and insisted that the projects were fine as we were inspecting them weekly at our regular status meetings. I insisted and Jack grudgingly agreed to take on this assignment.

RULE # 2

Put numbers on everything

RULE # 3

Red Yellow Green it
with clear success criteria

The next morning, Jack walked in sheepishly and showed me the dashboard. We had many reds and a few yellows on the dashboard. We were headed towards multiple train wrecks! My instinct was right after all. Jack asked if he still had a job, and I emphatically said "Yes! Otherwise who is going to clean this up for us? Me?"

Dashboards Killed The Drama

We decided that it was important to have a dashboard process that measured regularly and consistently. Jack agreed to the following new activities:

• Take measurements or collect data every Friday and publish the dashboard each Monday.

• Assign a score and rate everything on a scale, even the subjective items.

• Display the dashboard publicly on his door.

• Work with his project managers to develop individual project dashboards for every customer project in our company.

RULE # 4

Display publicly

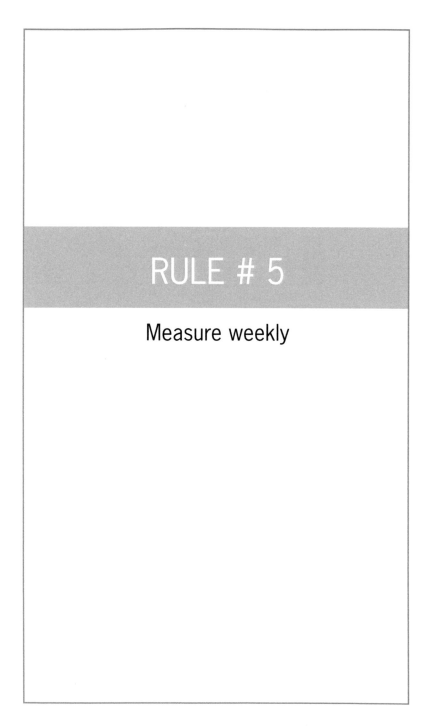

RULE # 5

Measure weekly

Jack was initially taken aback by the idea of displaying these dashboards in public, especially since there were so many reds and yellows. He felt embarrassed and was concerned that the detailed dashboards would also embarrass his project managers. Jack pleaded, "Why don't we fix these problems first, then display these dashboards publicly? That way we won't scare or upset other team members." I assured him that embarrassing him or anyone else was not my agenda. My agenda was to arrive at the best solutions to our problems in the fastest possible time.

If we attempted to fix the problems before displaying the dashboards, we would only have two brains working on these problems. If we displayed the dashboards immediately, we would be able to activate all fifty brains in the consulting group to work on these problems. The idea of tapping into the power of our collective intelligence provided Jack with the courage to display these dashboards publicly.

Jack's initial reaction to fix problems before displaying the dashboards publicly is very typical and logical. Unfortunately it stemmed from self-preservation, fear and embarrassment. These are powerful ingredients that put drama into companies. Drama creeps in from three main areas: people and emotions, subjectivity, and the lack of candor.

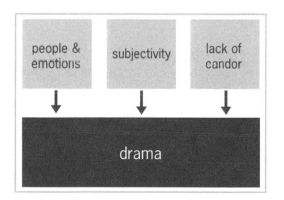

So what's the big deal? The big deal is that drama causes the following situations that typically lead to disastrous results:

• Focusing on the wrong issues

• Missed opportunities

• Putting the wrong people in the wrong seats to make people happy

In contrast, publicly displayed dashboards will provide the exact opposite environment:

• Focus on the right issues and not people

• A system designed for candid conversations to solve problems

• Faster solutions, decisions and ultimately larger profits

Dashboard Monday

That Monday the dashboards went up on everyone's doors.

It was the best thing we could have done. I explained to my team that my objective was neither to berate nor to place blame.

The initial dashboard was our baseline. **It did not matter how we got to our baseline. Only what we chose to do moving forward truly mattered.** I encouraged every single team member to figure out how we could collectively drive our dashboard status from reds and yellows to greens. When I look back now I can say in hindsight "Hey! We chose to focus on the problems, not the people". Back then it just seemed practical. If I got angry with all the people, who would be left to solve the problems?

RULE # 6

Focus on the problems,
not the people

By framing the initial dashboards as a baseline to work from and improve, people were not embarrassed by the red indices on their dashboards. In fact, it was almost like receiving a "get out of jail free" card. Instead, we all focused on getting the reds to improve to greens. A flurry of activity broke out - meetings, discussions, solutions, and suggestions. For the next few months, I did two things consistently. First, I ensured that these dashboards were done and up on everyone's door by Monday morning without exception. Second, I walked down the hallway and studied them. Over the next few months, most of the red and yellow indices turned to green. We had turned our projects around in a very short time.

Tip:
Displaying the dashboards on doors and walls was a critical decision towards our ultimate success. They became a communication vehicle and the catalyst for fast action.

Our initial success with dashboards in the consulting group prompted the rest of the company to take action as well. These dashboards spread like wildfire. Soon, with some assistance from me, every department had dashboards up that provided them with the same insight that the consulting group had gained.

RULE # 7

Give everybody a
"get out of jail free" card
when the baseline dashboard
is displayed

RULE # 8

Make it a helpful and actionable tool,
not a management club

Benefits

As the CEO, I now had my finger on the pulse of the company. I had an early warning system that helped to prevent potential train wrecks. Our teams had the same insight and took the right actions without being managed.

These dashboards changed our activities, discussions, and ultimately the culture of our company. *We became more team centric, candid and results driven.* We became more accountable to ourselves as well as our teammates. Our work culture progressed in a number of ways:

- **Vibrant team meetings.** Status meetings changed from spending 75% of the time discussing status, to only 10%, with the rest of the time spent on brainstorming solutions to problems.

- **Wisdom of teams.** These dashboards provided a communication vehicle for teams to discuss and come up with solutions together instead of individuals solving problems themselves.

- **Candor.** Specific criteria made subjective areas more objective. This objectivity naturally encouraged candor as the dashboards focused us on problems and helped us not to attack individual team members.

- **Accountability.** People understood which areas they were responsible for. By having to report their status weekly on a dashboard posted on their door, team members naturally took ownership over their areas.

- **Sharpened our focus.** The dashboards reminded us of what was most important as new initiatives threatened to distract our attention to other things.

Lessons Learned

Upon reflection, and with the benefit of building a good number of dashboards since that time, I have the following observations to share:

- You have heard that "what gets measured gets done". True! But how do you know what to measure? Measuring the wrong things is even worse than not measuring.

- Simple and fewer measurements get you better and quicker results.

- Dashboards harness the collective intelligence of a team. They must be displayed publicly for teams to use as the catalyst to discuss, brainstorm, and take action to solve problems.

- It takes energy and drive to enforce a process over time that develops the right habits within an organization.

- The dashboard with the right and meaningful information drives performance and accountability. By the same token, the wrong dashboards with irrelevant indices create exasperation and frustration.

- The right candid conversations need to happen around a dashboard. Stay focused on attacking problems. Stay away from attacking people.

- Dashboards guide a company's execution by: (1) reinforcing goals and success criteria; (2) providing weekly feedback on progress that is being made towards the goals; and (3) improving overall communication on the issues by removing the subjectivity and the emotion from the process.

RULE # 9

Less is more

And Now...
there's SuperGreen™

"It's ok if you aim for the sky and hit the trees,
but it's not ok to aim for the trees and hit the ground."
~Patrick Thean

Reward and Celebrate Super Results

Verne Harnish and I were discussing this book when he asked me this question: "What if someone totally blew away his or her goal, how would you account for this on your dashboard?" Verne felt that it was inaccurate to represent such super performance with "green". We needed another color to document, motivate and celebrate fantastic results.

We brainstormed on this for a while and came up with the concept of SuperGreen™. SuperGreen™ is the celebration of super results. SuperGreen™ should be reserved for communicating and celebrating results that are truly great. Do not feel compelled to have a SuperGreen™ rating. On the contrary, you should have a very compelling reason to even have SuperGreen™ on your dashboard.

Tip:
A common mistake is to reward superhuman efforts with a SuperGreen™ score regardless of results achieved. Use SuperGreen™ ONLY to reward super results, not superhuman effort.

The criteria for SuperGreen™ should be determined and communicated at the beginning of projects no differently from the other success criteria. If you do this, you will motivate your team to aim for the sky instead of aiming for the trees.

We recently achieved SuperGreen™ by helping a client sell his business for a premium. It was exciting! I look forward to sharing that story with you in "Selling Your Business For A Premium", the next book in the Red Yellow Green Series.

Summary

"A journey of a thousand miles begins with a single step."
~Confucius

The Bottom Line

The right dashboards will allow you to see problems before they smack you in the face by helping you to manage your business proactively in these ways:

• Timely decisions by measuring and displaying the right metrics

• Provide you with insight into the future to avoid being blindsided

• Align your team behind common goals, with a common tool and using a common language

• Change or move your company culture towards accountability and problem solving

Our Journey Continues With Leadline, LLC.

Metasys began my journey into dashboards. Since then, I have built numerous dashboards for friends and clients. I was compelled to establish Leadline and focus on helping growth companies compete and win in a flat world. Global competition brings both opportunities and

challenges, as described by Tom Friedman in his book "The World Is Flat". How will companies compete and win in this global economy? The answer is to have the right headlights (future vision) to see both opportunities and challenges that may be coming up around the bend.

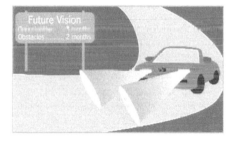

I would be thrilled to hear about your successes. Please e-mail me at patrick@leadline.com.

I end with a wish for you - that our 9 Simple Rules for Dashboarding will provide you with the right headlights and help to ensure your company's bright future!

9 Simple Rules
For Dashboarding™

*"Each problem that I solved became a rule
which served afterwards to solve other problems."*
~Rene Descartes

Rule # 1

Start with
the right questions

Rule # 2

Put numbers on
everything

Rule # 3

Red Yellow Green it
with clear
success criteria

Rule # 4

Display publicly

Rule # 5

Measure weekly

Rule # 6

Focus on the problems,
not the people

Rule # 7

Give everybody a
"get out of jail free"
card when the baseline
dashboard is displayed

Rule # 8

Make it a helpful
and actionable tool,
not a management club

Rule # 9

Less is more

The
Red Yellow Green Tool™

"He who every morning plans the transaction of the day and follows out that plan, carries a thread that will guide him through the maze of the most busy life. But where no plan is laid, where the disposal of time is surrendered merely to the chance of incidence, chaos will soon reign."
~Victor Hugo
French dramatist, novelist, & poet (1802 - 1885)

1 Goals

#1:_____

_____

Who:_____

When:_____

#2:_____

_____

Who:_____

When:_____

#3:_____

_____

Who:_____

When:_____

2 #1: Success Criteria

● Min:_____
○ Yellow: Between Min and Goal
○ Goal:_____
● SuperGreen™:_____

3 #2: Success Criteria

● Min:_____
○ Yellow: Between Min and Goal
○ Goal:_____
● SuperGreen™:_____

4 #3: Success Criteria

● Min:_____
○ Yellow: Between Min and Goal
○ Goal:_____
● SuperGreen™:_____

Notes

Notes

Notes

Execution Without The Drama

Order Form

Execution Without The Drama™
by Patrick Thean

Price: $14.95 (10 books or more, $9.95 each)

Quantity:

Total: $

Signature: Date:

Name on Card:

Billing Address:

Phone: Email:

Credit Card #:

Expiration Date: CVC Code:

To place order:
- cut and mail form to 813 E. Kingston Ave. Charlotte, NC 28203
- or fax form to 980.297.7701
- or visit www.RedYellowGreenSeries.com to order on-line